POCKET

tangles

POCKET CREATIVES

F

FRANCES LINCOLN LIMITED

PUBLISHERS

The Zentangle® Method is an easy-to-learn, relaxing, and fun way to create beautiful images by drawing structured patterns. It was created by Rick Roberts and Maria Thomas. *Zentangle* is a registered trademark of Zentangle, Inc. Learn more at zentangle.com.

Practising tangles is an important part of the process and *Pocket Tangles* has been designed to give you the perfect place to do that. Once you have discovered a particular tangle that you like (and there are many resources on the internet) you can practice it here or combine it with others to create your unique tangle design.

Whether you are looking to tangle in the traditional tile, create a mandala or go freeform, *Pocket Tangles* is the place to do that. You can create a visual directory of your favourite tangles in 'My Tangle Directory' at the back of the book.

MY TANGLE DIRECTORY

Verdigogh

Yincut

Pepper

Squid

Huggins

Knights Bridge

Hollibaugh

MY TANGLE DIRECTORY

MY TANGLE DIRECTORY

Frances Lincoln Limited
74–77 White Lion Street, London N1 9PF
www.franceslincoln.com

Pocket Tangles
Copyright © Frances Lincoln Limited 2014

First Frances Lincoln edition 2014

A catalogue record for this book is available
from the British Library.

ISBN 978-0-7112-3556-4

Printed and bound in China

9 8 7 6 5 4 3 2 1